The **Drawing** Book

Leon Baxter

IDEALS CHILDREN'S BOOKS

Library of Congress controlling-in-publication data

Baxter, Leon.
The drawing book.

Summary: Gives instruction on using depth,
perspective, shading, and proportion in drawing animals,
people, landscapes, and nature.
1. Drawing-Technique-Juvenile Literature.
[1. Drawing-Technique] 1. Title.
NC730.836 1990   741.2   90-4476
ISBN 0-8249-8475-7

First published in the United States by
Ideals Publishing Corporation
Nelson Place at Elm Hill Pike
Nashville, Tennessee 37214

First published in Great Britain by
William Collins Sons and Co., Ltd.
in association with Belitha Press, Ltd.
London, England

Text and illustrations in this format copyright © 1990 by Belitha Press, Ltd.

Text and illustrations copyright © 1988 by Leon Baxter and the estate of
Colin Caket

LET'S DRAW is based on the LET'S DRAW series originally published by
Collins/Belitha in 1988 and 1989

ISBN 0-8249-8475-7

Typesetting by Chambers Wallace
London, England

Printed and bound in Hong Kong for Imago Publishing

CONTENTS

Drawing is fun, so why not join in! This book is designed to help you put on paper the things you see around you and the things you see in your mind. There is no *right* way to draw – every artist has his or her own way of doing things. So don't be afraid to try. Use this book to help you find the way *you* like to draw and to give you some hints about what makes a picture "work."

The Drawing Book begins with the basics of drawing – how to make pictures with numbers and picture squares – and then moves on to more involved exercises, such as drawing people and animals and illustrating action. Take as much time as you need in practicing the basics, and don't worry if your picture does not turn out exactly as you wanted. Try again. Remember, it's much better to make lots of practice drawings than to try to make a perfect picture right away.

The more you draw and the better you become with drawing, the more you will want to draw. Experiment! Use crayons and paint together and see what happens. Instead of coloring an area with just one colored pencil, try two or more, or mix your pencil lines with areas of felt-tip color. There are all sorts of things you can try.

As you make more and more pictures, your drawings will improve. Look at the pictures you like best and decide *why* you like them. Then use this information in your future drawings.

But above all, have fun!

You will need:

pencils	colored pencils
crayons	paints
pastels	felt-tip pens
tracing paper	lots of drawing paper (white and colored)

Have a good time!

Leon Baxter

Making Faces

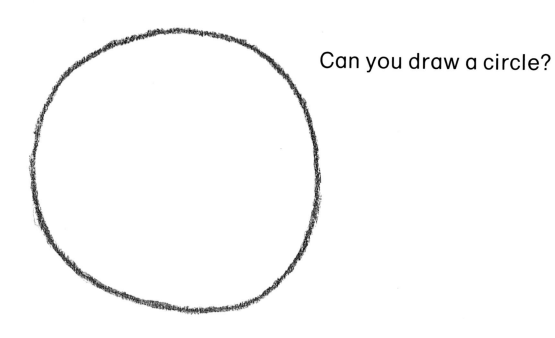

Can you draw a circle?

Now make it smile.

Paint it yellow like the sun.

Try making circle faces on your paper.
Add ears and hair and funny hats.

8

This is a happy frog.

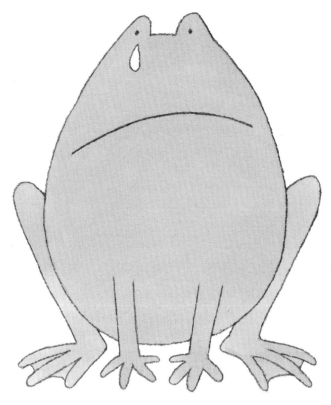

This is a sad frog.

This frog is puzzled.

This frog is laughing.

Notice how the shapes of the eyes and mouth change when feelings change.

9

This monkey is sad.

This monkey is happy.

This monkey is laughing.

This monkey is shouting.

Draw your own monkey faces.

10

Sally is . . .

sleeping

crying

eating

angry

Can you draw your own people with different faces?

Number
and
Word Pictures

If you can draw one . . .

you can have some fun!

tree

tent

candle

boat

Different numbers make it easier to draw different kinds of things.

If you can
do a two . . .

you can draw
a swan!

What can *you* make with a figure 3?

16

If you can make a six . . .

you can draw a pelican. Now you try.

18

19

If you can make an eight . . .

you can make a cat . . .

or a frog!

Now you try.

20

Make a nine into a can.

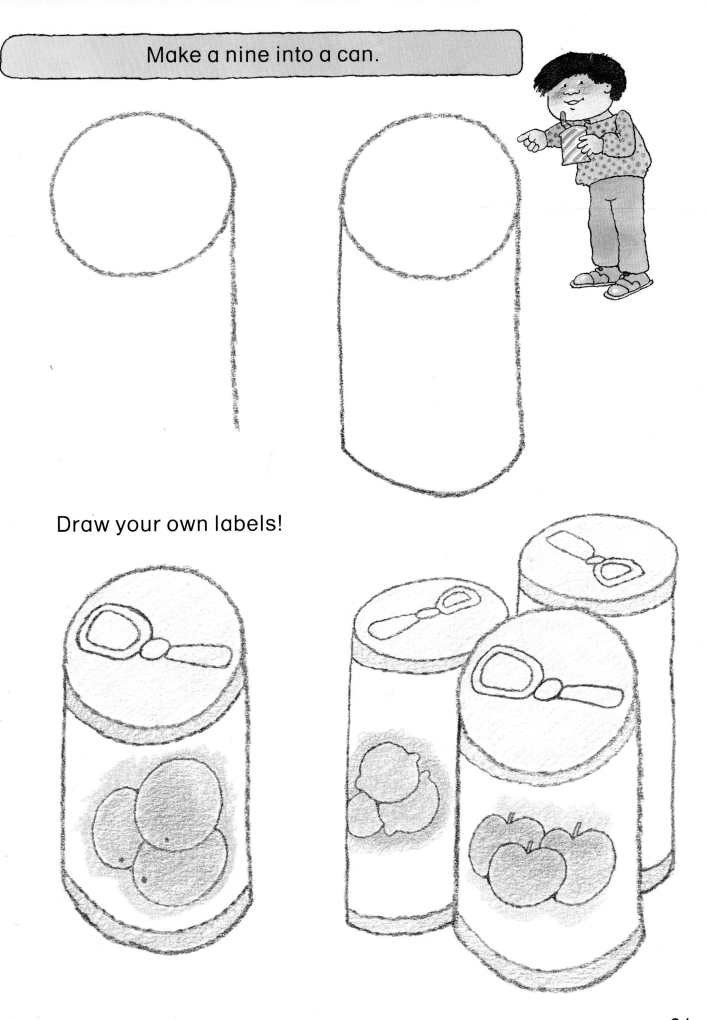

Draw your own labels!

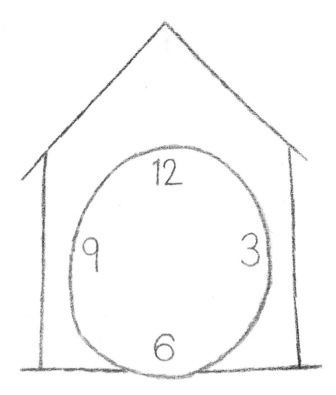

Time for you to try.

Leon Baxter

Can you write your name in pictures?

Helpful Squares

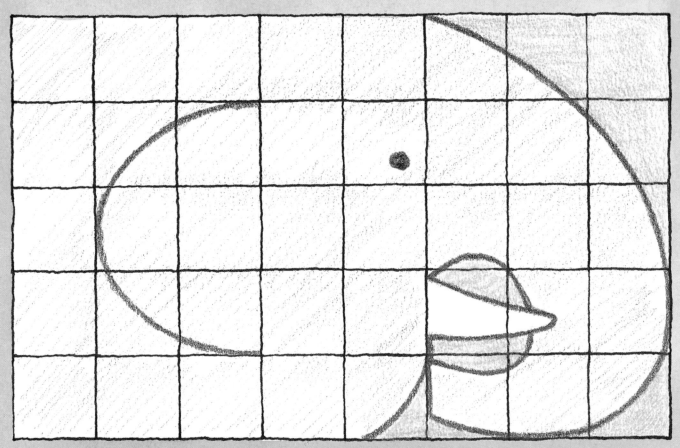

Here is a picture of an elephant, drawn with picture squares.
Trace these blank squares on a separate sheet of paper.

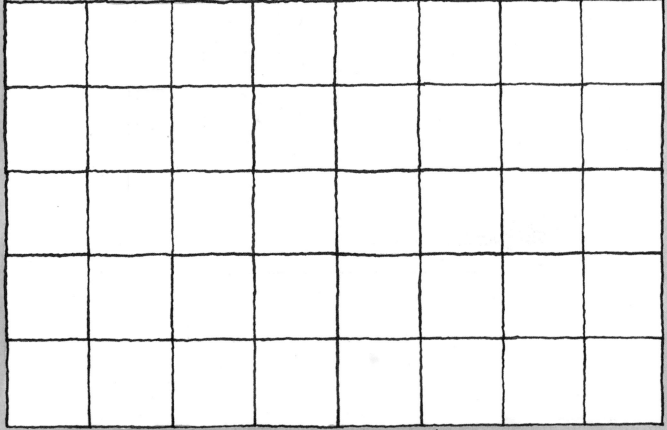

Use these squares as a guide to help you draw your
own elephant.

25

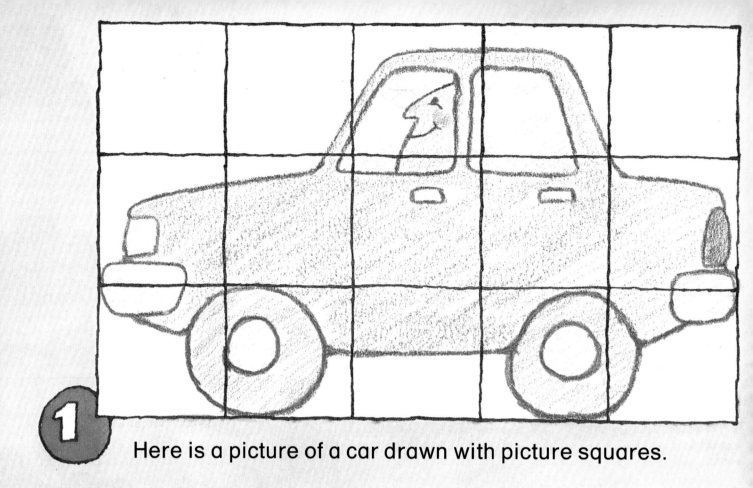

Here is a picture of a car drawn with picture squares.

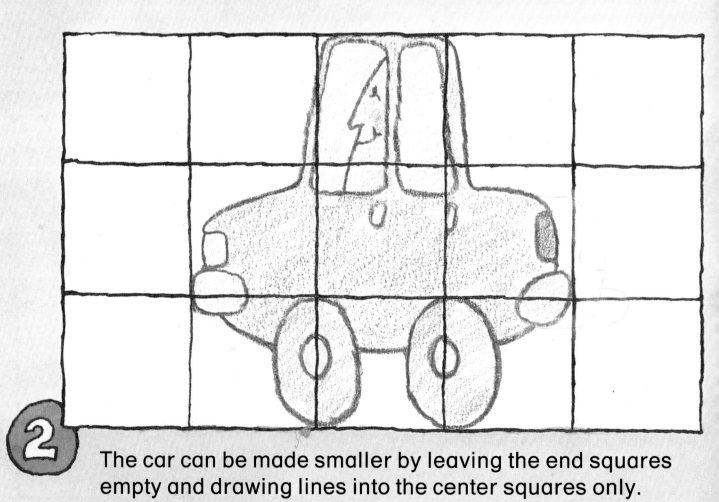

2 The car can be made smaller by leaving the end squares empty and drawing lines into the center squares only.

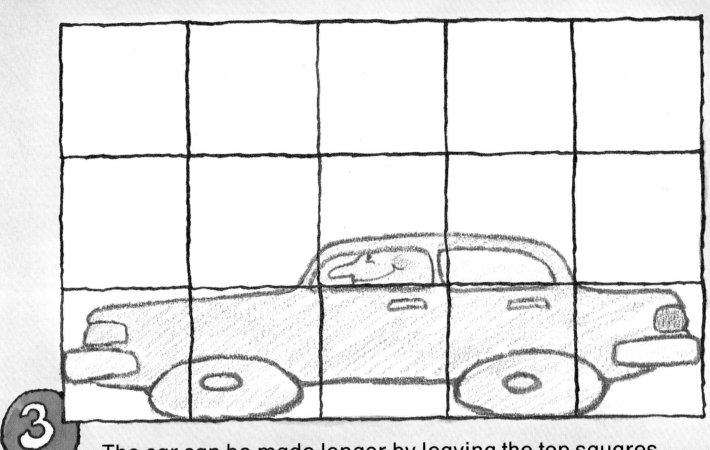

3 The car can be made longer by leaving the top squares empty and drawing lines into the bottom squares only.

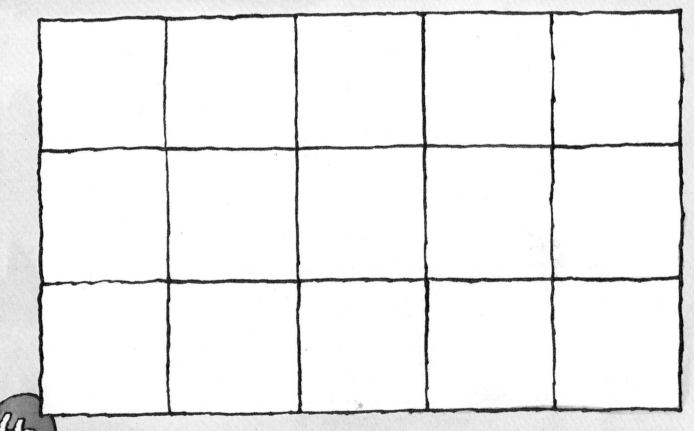

4 Now trace these squares and use them to draw the car the way *you* like it.

1 Here is a picture of an elephant.

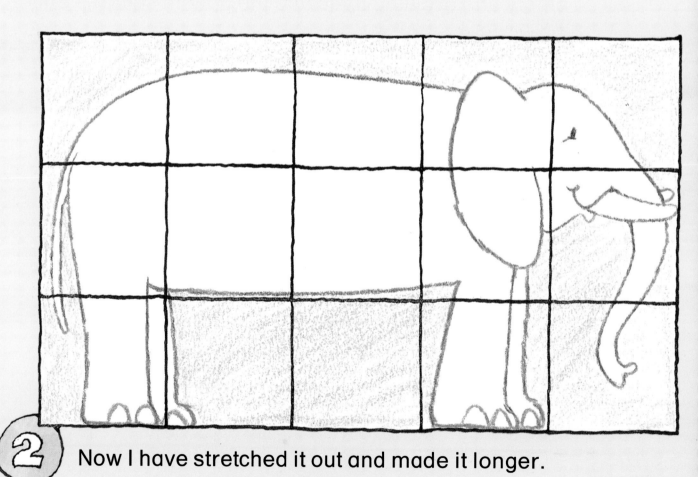

2 Now I have stretched it out and made it longer.

28

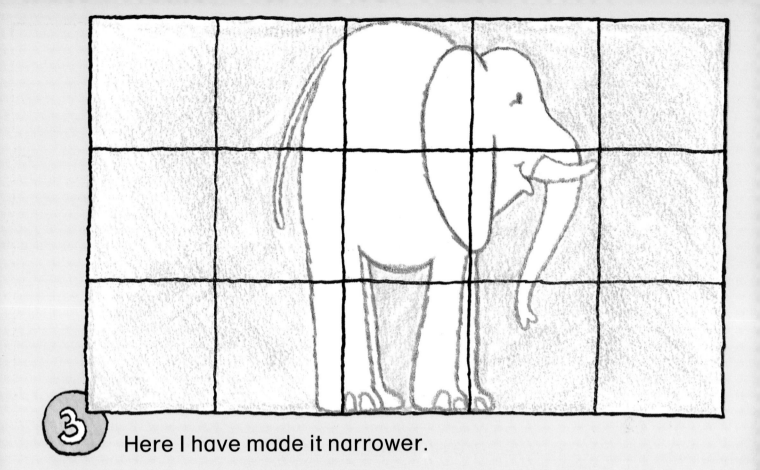

3 Here I have made it narrower.

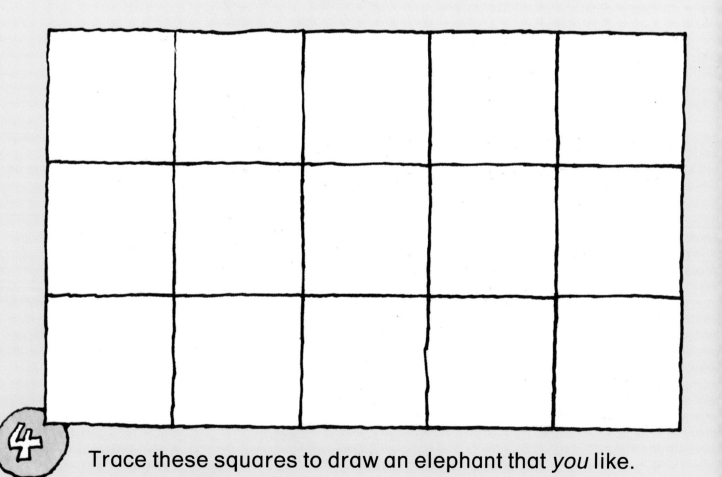

4 Trace these squares to draw an elephant that *you* like.

Shapes in Nature

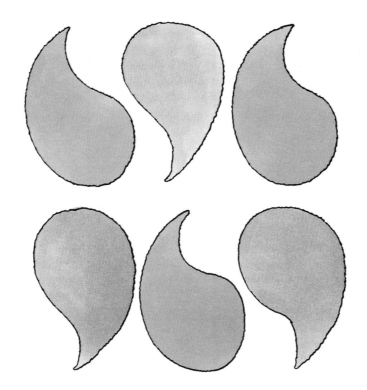

Rainfall

Rainfall is a part of nature's well-designed plan. The sun shining over the sea makes water rise and form clouds. The clouds then move over the land where the water falls from the clouds as rain. Clouds come in all shapes and sizes.

Clouds and rain are fun to draw.

Look at all these cloud shapes.

Now draw your own.

When raindrops fall, they are heavier at the bottom and so they form beautiful tear shapes.

Tear shapes make good patterns.

Design some tear patterns of your own.

Once it has fallen as rain, water has to get back to the sea. Little streams come together to form rivers.

Water can not flow uphill or through mountains, so it has to find a way around them.

Flowing water makes sweeping, curving shapes.

33

Rivers

Rivers can be fast and noisy or slow and lazy. This is a slow, meandering river. Try drawing a river with some trees reflected in the water.

Mountains

I live in the mountains.

Mountains rise high into the sky.

Draw them as separate, huge shapes. The peaks behind are far away.

Some mountains are snow-capped and some hide their heads in the clouds. Can you draw a mountain range with snow and clouds?

Flowers and plants

Flowers send their roots down to drink water and absorb nutrients. They send their leaves and petals up and out to catch the sunshine. Even though all flowers obey these rules, they come in many different shapes, sizes, and colors.

rose

tulip

I have drawn two flowers.

Like flowers, trees send their roots down and their leaves and limbs up and out. And trees, too, grow in different shapes and sizes – some are broad and flat and some are thin and pointed.

oak

yew

I have drawn two leaves.

Can you draw your favourite flowers and leaves?

Often plants are made up of small shapes that form together to make larger, symmetrical shapes.

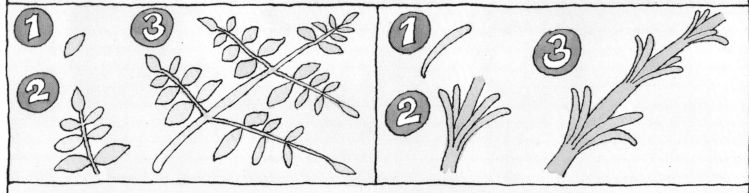

Sometimes little flowers grow closely together to form multi-flowered heads.

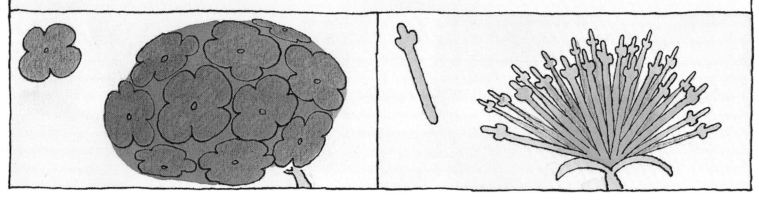

Can you draw groups of plants together? Think of the ways they might lean and bend.

Look around you. What color is a tree?

Some trees are green in summer

. . . but turn red later.

Others turn yellow instead.

Some stay green all year!

Some tree trunks are grey, some are mossy green, and a few are brown.
Can you draw a tree scene?

Space
and
Depth

Skyline pictures

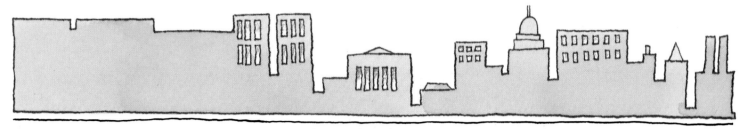

Without lifting your pencil or brush from the paper, draw a line like this:

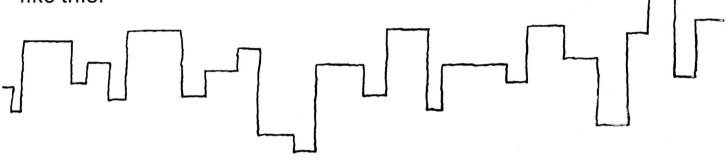

Add towers, roofs, domes, and windows.

Try it again using more than one line.

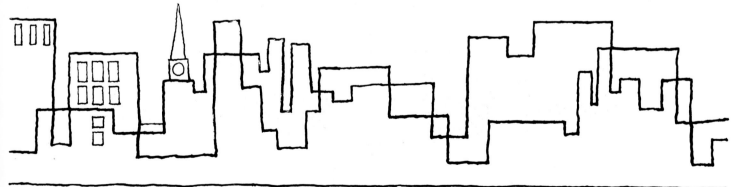

Can you draw some skylines of your own?

Outdoor scenes

Look around you and see that some things are near you while others are far away. This is space and depth. Objects in pictures appear either closer or farther away by creating illusions.

The illusion of space is created by drawing an *eye level* in your scene. Your eye level will depend upon how you see the scene. Notice how the artist above changes his eye level as he changes his position. What you see straight ahead of you is your eye level.

Depth is created by establishing a *vanishing point*. The vanishing point is a single spot at eye level. In the drawings above, notice how the road appears to disappear at the vanishing point. If the lines on your drawing angle toward the vanishing point, you will create this illusion of depth. Notice how the lines beside the road in the right-hand drawing become shorter as they near the vanishing point – their lines are angled toward it! You would create fences, buildings, and telephone poles in the same way.

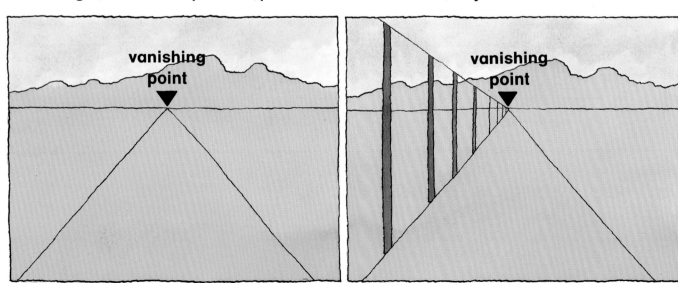

Distant colors

When you look into the distance,
colors seem to fade.

Which areas look close to you and which areas look far away?

A red car sets off down the road.
The color of the car appears to fade as it moves away.

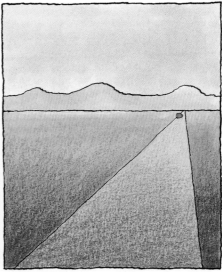

Now you choose two colors. Can you create close-looking areas
and distant-looking areas?

The city

Choose your own eye level and vanishing point and draw a city. If you move your eye level down, the buildings will look taller.

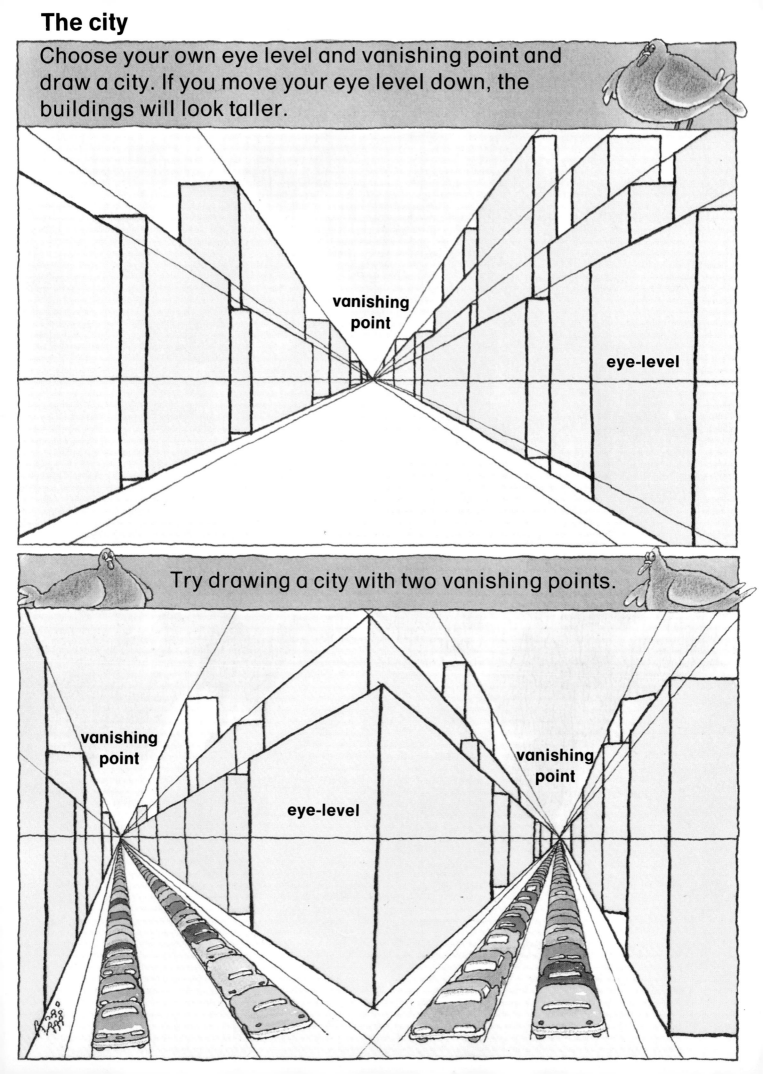

vanishing point

eye-level

Try drawing a city with two vanishing points.

vanishing point

eye-level

vanishing point

Drawing People

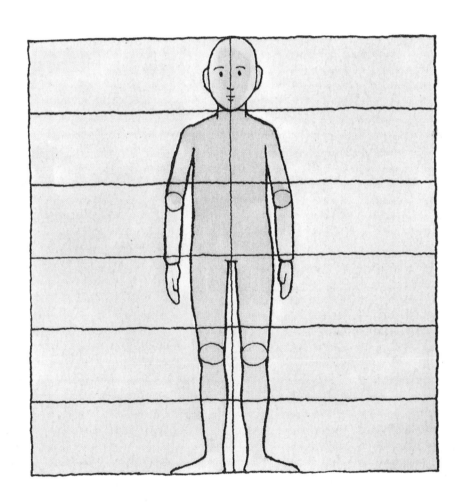

This section is about drawing people. To do this, we have to know about the proportions and measurements of the body.

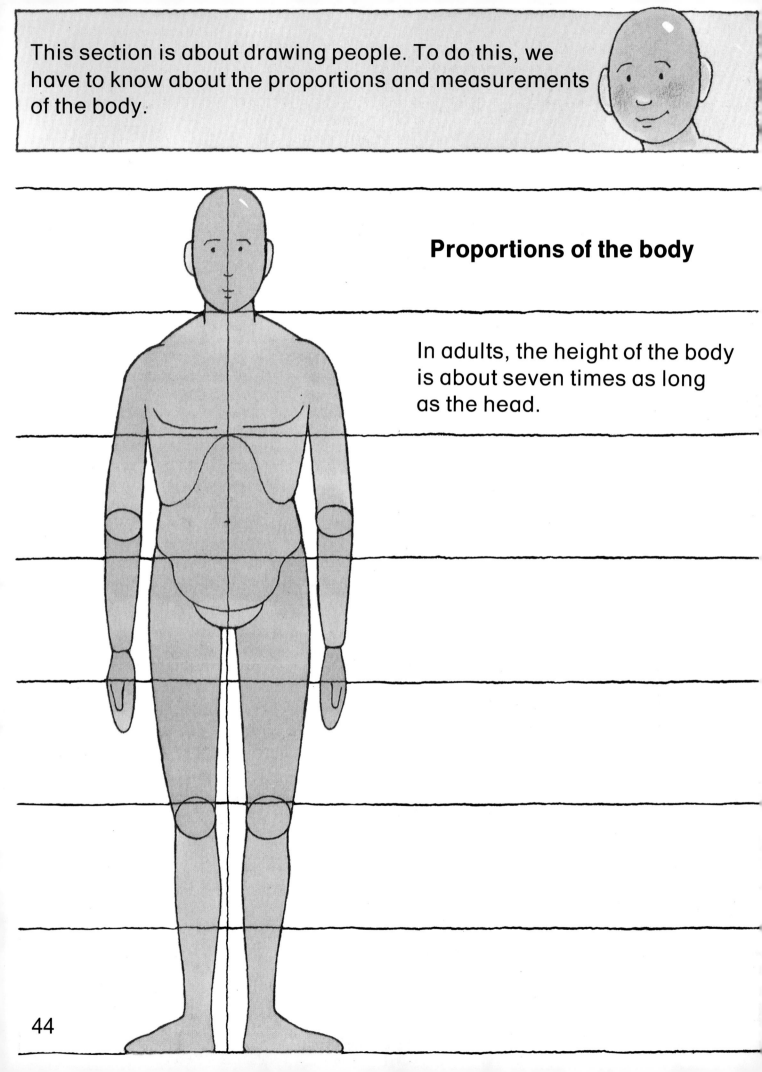

Proportions of the body

In adults, the height of the body is about seven times as long as the head.

In a baby, the height of the body is about four times as long as the head.

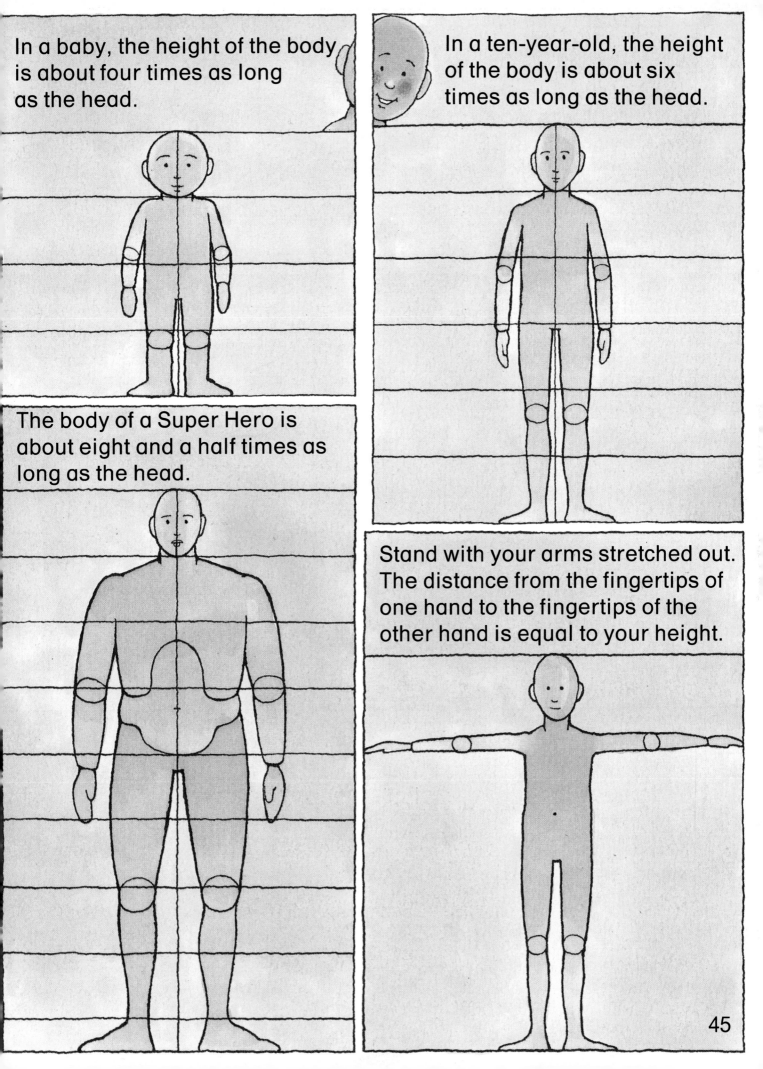

In a ten-year-old, the height of the body is about six times as long as the head.

The body of a Super Hero is about eight and a half times as long as the head.

Stand with your arms stretched out. The distance from the fingertips of one hand to the fingertips of the other hand is equal to your height.

Proportions *do* vary, so find a model and do some measuring for yourself.

Use your pencil as a measuring tool.

Hold your pencil as shown.

You can slide your thumb up and down.

Keep your arm straight and hold up your pencil or brush. By moving your thumb up and down, you can find the height of your model's head.

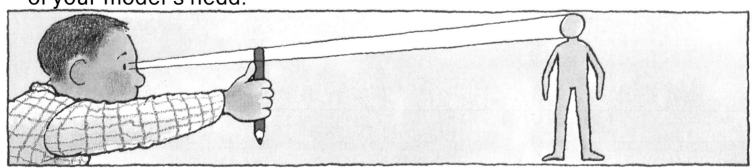

Hold up your pencil or brush so that the top is in line with the top of the model's head.

Now slide your thumb so that the tip of your thumb is in line with the chin.

head height

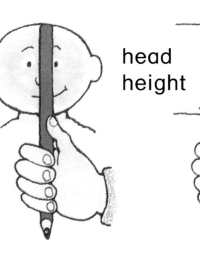

Keep your thumb still and your pencil or brush upright; use the head as a unit of measurement and find out how many times the head will go into your model's body.

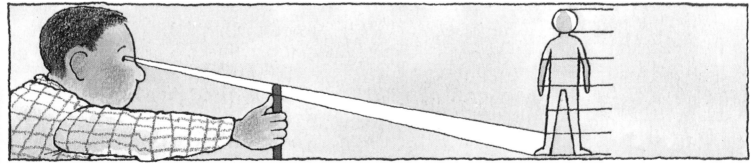

Look at your family and friends and make pictures of them.

Proportions of the head

Ears are aligned with eyebrows at the top, and the tip of the nose at the bottom.

The hairline is about one-third down from the top of the head to the eyes.

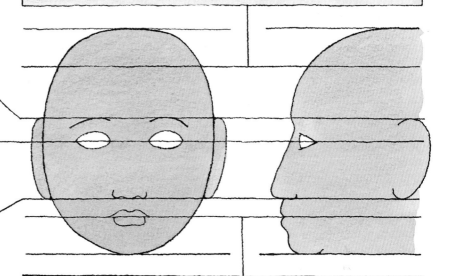

Eyes are halfway down the head.

The tip of the nose is halfway between the eyes and the chin.

The mouth is about one-third of the way between the nose and the chin.

Follow these guidelines when you want to draw a head which is turned away from you.

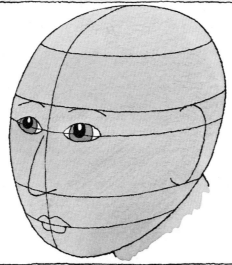

By laying your pencil on a drawing, you can use your forefinger and thumb to measure and check distances.

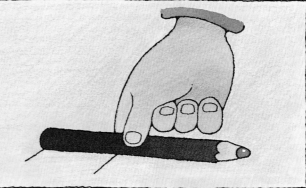

Hands and feet

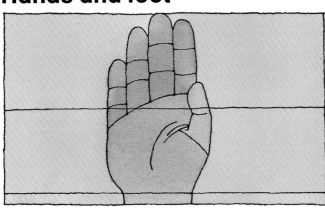

Look at your hand and see where the tip of each finger is in relation to the others. Notice the shape and position of the thumb.

Can you draw these hands?

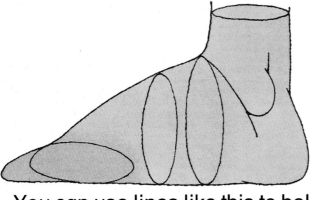

Look at the shape of a foot. See how it flattens out towards the end.

These are construction lines.

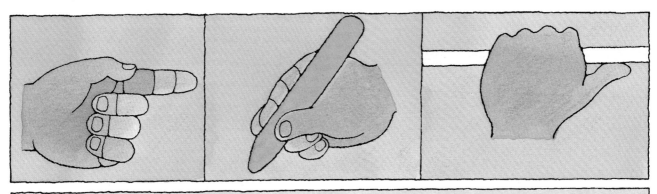

You can use lines like this to help you learn about the shape of a foot.

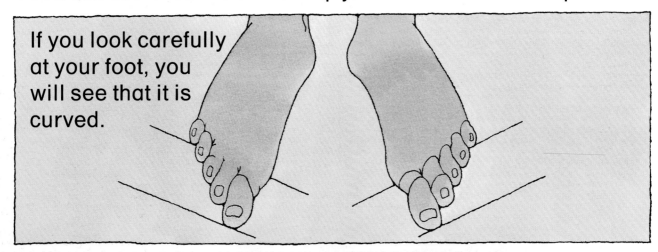

If you look carefully at your foot, you will see that it is curved.

Foreshortening

You can draw someone by using cylinders as the parts of the body.

Turn a cylinder towards you and it appears to grow shorter. This is called foreshortening.

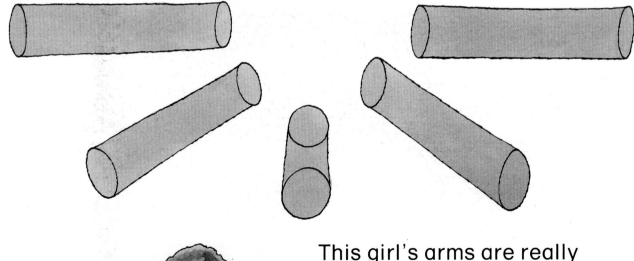

This girl's arms are really the same length. Her left arm is coming towards you but because of its position it looks as if it is shorter.

Weight watching

When drawing people, there are many factors to consider, such as their weight, height, and overall size. How do you begin?

The boy in picture A is our model. Let's ignore details like face and clothes and make a basic drawing showing *how* he is sitting.

The arrows show where his weight is being supported.

I have imagined his spine and I have drawn a frame for building my picture.

I add the other arm and the legs.

Now I can add flesh with cylinders.

Try drawing some cylinder people.

Making a portrait gallery

Try drawing fun portraits of your family and friends using what you have learned. These are two of my favorite relatives.

Aunt Battren   Uncle Baldwin

Drawing
Animals

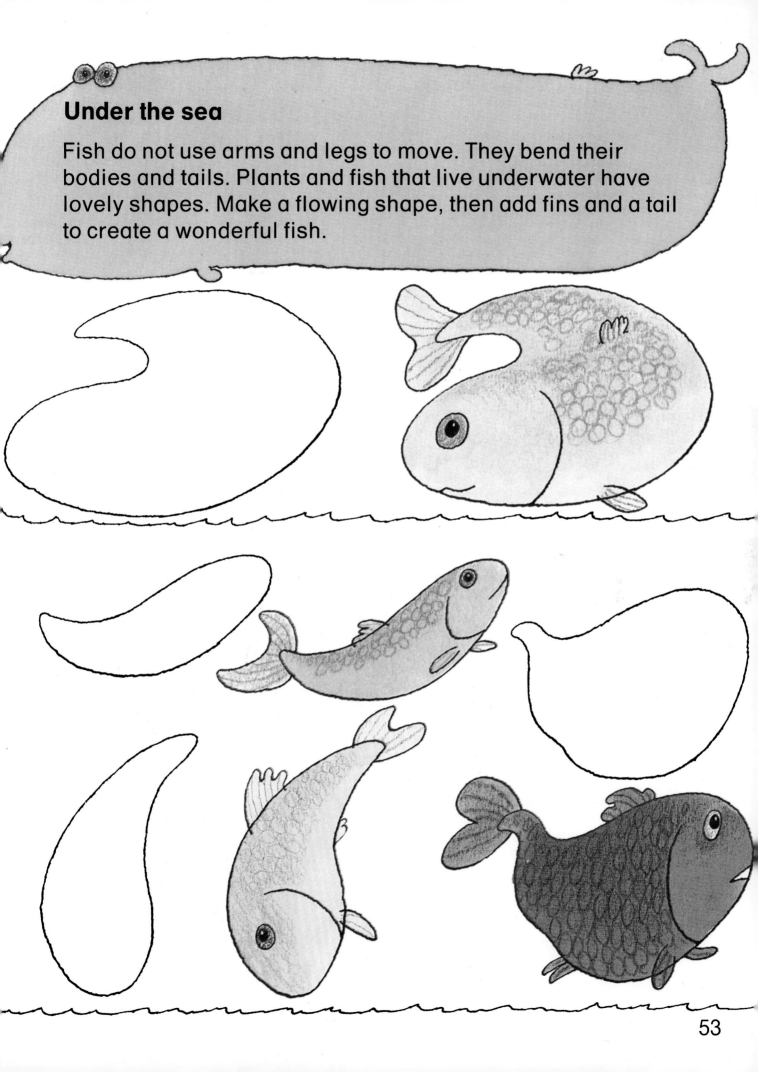

Under the sea

Fish do not use arms and legs to move. They bend their bodies and tails. Plants and fish that live underwater have lovely shapes. Make a flowing shape, then add fins and a tail to create a wonderful fish.

Dogs
I have used simple shapes to draw this dog and its puppies.

Cats
Look at the shapes I have used to draw a cat and kittens.

Try drawing some of your own dogs and cats.

Birds

Birds have skeletons similar to ours. This girl is standing as if she were a bird.

Birds have two fingers and a thumb within the structure of their wings.

Birds stand on their toes. Most birds have three front toes and one back toe.

They have deep chests for the powerful muscles that move their wings.

Try drawing birds of different sizes.

55

Many animals stand on their toes. Their skeletons are similar to ours, but their joints are in different places.

The top half of a horse's limbs are part of its body.

elbow

knee

This boy is standing as if he were a horse.

The knee is our wrist.

heel

knee

The hock is our heel.

If a horse stood like you, it would look like this.

Now you try to draw a horse.

Action

Action!

Here is a picture sequence.
It tells an action story.

The action is shown by bending and stretching lines and by
drawing something either about to happen or that has happened.
This gives the suggestion of time.

How to suggest time

In these three pictures we can show:

before

1. He is going to kick the ball.

during

2. He is kicking the ball.

after

3. He has kicked the ball.

before

1. She is going to throw the ball.

during

2. She is throwing the ball.

after

3. She has thrown the ball.

Can you make up your own sequence pictures?

Action sequences

Look at these two picture sequences. One series of actions takes place in a short space of time, while the other is over a much longer period.

By changing backgrounds and showing means of travel, you can suggest time passing. Now draw your own vacation sequence.

Moviemaking

These men are filming a stuntman driving a car over a cliff.

Create your own favorite action scene in four frames.

INDEX